When God Sent My Husband

Wisdoms for Capturing and Keeping a Man's Heart

RAINIE HOWARD
PATRICK HOWARD

ISBN-10: 1518709613
ISBN-13: 978-1518709616

TABLE OF CONTENTS

❖

ACKNOWLEDGEMENTS

To my Lord and Savior Jesus Christ
To my loving husband Patrick
To my beautiful children, Patrick "Bj" and Aniyah

Thank you and I love you.

INTRODUCTION

❖

Have you found yourself in the midst of a broken heart or tarnished as a result of loving someone with your entire body, heart and soul only to be left more broken than ever? Has your dream of a fairy-tale marriage been destroyed by the reality of your poverty of love?

It happens when you cherish a man with all your precious heart, giving him all your hidden treasures in hopes of receiving the undeniable, that everlasting unconditional love never arrives. The love isn't present because he was never present. He was always distant, distant in heart and spirit. This is a major problem because you envision yourself in the arms of your loving husband feeling safe and secure. You see yourself in a loving relationship with the man of your dreams. In your imagination, you've walked down that aisle in your beautiful white wedding gown too many times to still be single. You can relate to the many women who've experienced heartache and pain from a devastating break up or a messy divorce. Regardless of where you are in your experience of love, this book will empower you to:

- Overcome rejection and restore your heart
- Heal from past heartbreak
- Learn to love before falling in love
- Allow God to be the matchmaker (Mark 10:9)
- Guard your heart while dating
- Prevent yourself from attracting predators
- Avoid deception from wolves in sheep's clothing
- Capture and keep a man's heart

Becoming a wife is not about being the prettiest, smartest, richest and most successful woman...it's about showing up. When you show up, you need to be ready at the right time with an open and pure heart. You must prepare yourself to receive love. This book is your complete guide to spiritual dating, which is to keep God at the center of all that you do in preparation for marriage. God is the ultimate matchmaker; "Therefore what God has joined together, let no one separate." (Mark 10:9)

The bible states that God should be involved in the joining of husband and wife. I'm often shocked when I hear people say it's not necessary to pray regarding dating, or they may say, "God is not a matchmaker, He gives us the free will to marry whomever we want to marry." Although God does give us free will, the bible says, "Be anxious for nothing but in all things through prayer and supplication with thanksgiving let your requests be known to God." (Philippians 4:6)

God is saying come to him about all things (dating, marriage etc...). If God wanted you to pick your own spouse without His input, then why would the bible say, "...lean not unto your own understanding. In all your ways acknowledge Him and He will direct your path." (Proverbs 3:6)

Your job is to seek God and not just for a week, a month or a year, but always. Diligently seek and obey the Lord. Wait for His guidance and call on your life and relationship. You have a creator, a God who is Lord over your life. It's not about following your will--that doesn't work--but instead allowing God's will to be done in your life.

One of the most famous motivational speakers in the world said, "If you want a good life, good marriage and good career, you must become an excellent super achiever." When I first heard these words, I received and believed them. However, today I disagree; it's not about becoming great at achieving something; it's about persevering to fight the good fight of faith. Trusting God always no matter what the situation looks like. Even when you're tired, weak, broken and unsure, just endure. Keep obeying God, keep moving forward in the Holy Spirit and don't give up. No matter how weak you are, how broken you become, or how tired you feel, just keep going. Endure to the end. As hard as it may be, never stop following God. Your obedience will be rewarded in due season.

CHAPTER 1

CHASING A PREMATURE BLESSING

I thought he was fine and tall with smooth caramel skin. His hair was just right, nicely clean cut, and his eyes were hazel brown. I thought he was the cutest boy in my school. I watched him from afar; he was so popular. I daydreamed about him being my boyfriend. I watched as he joked with his friends, and his laugh and smile were very attractive to me.

After many days of having a secret crush on him, I finally gathered the courage to tell someone. Sitting in class, I turned to my friend Sherry, "Do you see him over there, the cute tall guy in the red shirt?"

"Yeah, I see him. Why, who is he?"

"That's Jordan and I really like him. I want to be his girlfriend. I need you to go up to him and ask him if he would go with me."

"Ok, I'll do it right now."

Immediately, my fourteen-year-old heart started racing. I was extremely nervous but hopeful at the same time. I was thinking of the strong desire I had to be loved by a man, but not just any man, the cutest boy in school who happened to be a seventeen-year-old junior in high school. I was a freshman but I was a risk-taker. I was ambitious and I wanted the best. At the same time I was very shy and quiet. I hid my personality. I was very insecure. I thought, finally he's going to know about me. Finally, the truth will come out and he will like me too. Maybe he will ask me to be his girl and we will live happily ever after. I was always a big dreamer but in this situation I was very optimistic. I thought, "Yes, I'm so happy she's going to tell him!"

And she did. I watched her walk up to Jordan. I could see her speaking to him while he listened. Then I saw her turn toward me pointing in my direction; he immediately looked at me. I quickly turned my head as if I had no idea what was going on. I didn't want him to see me looking at him. I looked away as if something else had my attention. The palm of my hands were sweating; I started breathing faster and faster as I felt my heart pounding out of my chest. In my mind I'm thinking, "what is he saying, what is he doing?"

One minute later Sherry came back to the table and sat next to me.

"Well, I told him."

I looked at her; my face was numb with a hint of excitement.

"What happened?"

"I told him you liked him, and I asked him would he ever go with you and he said, *never*."

My heart was crushed; the small amount of self-esteem in my soul had died in that very moment. I wasn't expecting this; I really didn't know what I expected. I just knew I was hurt. I was too speechless to respond. I wanted to cry but I didn't. How could he do this to me? This was the very first time I experienced rejection.

Seeking love

I was desperate for love. I needed love from a man. My Dad had spent most of my lifetime in prison, and the only memories I had of him were when I was five years old. I remember him cherishing me and showing me so much love when I was a little girl. He made me feel special, but it had been almost ten years since I seen him. I missed my Daddy; I really wanted him in my life. I was so embarrassed and ashamed to tell anyone he was in jail. Having my Dad locked up made me feel invaluable and less than. As a teenager I thought, "How could I be loved if my own father wouldn't get his life right, get off drugs and get out of prison and be in my life?" I was so empty and hurting for love. I just wanted to be held, kissed, hugged, and loved. Instead of being sad about not having my father in my life, I started focusing on finding my own love. Every morning I would pray for a boyfriend. I begged God to give me a boyfriend now. One day I heard the Holy Spirit say, "What if the right one isn't ready yet and it's not time, do you still want a boyfriend now?"

Chasing the idea of love

My hollow desperate soul said, "Yes, even if he's not the right one or it's not the right time, I still want a boyfriend now." In this particular season in my life, I didn't care if it was right or if it was God's will; I was so anxious to just have any form of "love" that it didn't matter if it were real love. I wanted to experience the physical, the kiss, the touch and the conversation I was longing for. I wanted to hear the words "I love you" and I didn't care about being in God's will and purpose. I had no idea how dangerous it was to be out of God's will. I had no clue about soul ties and the life-changing results of being unequally yoked with another person. I later discovered that the bible talks about souls being knit together and becoming one flesh. In 1 Corinthians 6:16, it says, "Or do you not know that he who is joined to a prostitute becomes one body with her? For, as it is written, the two will become one flesh."

I didn't know two souls could be joined together as one in the spiritual ream. While married couples can be drawn together like magnets, an abused woman can be joined spiritually to her abusive boyfriend and have no idea why she can't leave. It's a soul tie, and that's why she can't just walk away. It's spiritual. This is the very reason 1 Corinthians 6:18 says, "Flee from sexual immorality. Every other sin a person commits outside of their body, but the sexual immorality person sins against his own body.

I didn't know that I needed to discern the spirit of a person and be wise as a serpent and harmless as a dove. -Matthew 10:16

I didn't know any of these things, and personally I didn't care. I had a desperate rebellious spirit and I was determined to be in a relationship. Instead of me chasing God, I was chasing "my idea of love." I idolized having a man.

When you idolize something, you don't have to bow down and worship it. You could be idolizing something by constantly thinking about it, constantly daydreaming about it, and meditating on it. When you do these things, you're training yourself to focus on it. You train yourself to obsess over it.

I deceived myself into believing God was first in my life. I thought I didn't idolize anything above Him. I was wrong.

I was so blind to the reality that I idolized "having a man." I thought that because God gave me a vision to be married one day, I needed to meditate on it and fill my time thinking about it, chasing it, and making major plans to fulfill the vision of being in a relationship. I didn't know God didn't give me the "vision" to replace Him.

In addition to that, I felt cheated as if God owed me for not giving me a reliable Dad. I lacked something that no other little girl should ever lack--a father. I saw myself as a fatherless child who was abandoned. It hurt and I didn't want to experience the hurt anymore.

One day my friend Sherry called me and asked if I'd like to go with her to "The Castle", a roller skating-rink and party venue for teens on Friday night. I asked my mom and she said, "yes". Wow, I was shocked. My mom had a reputation for being a very strict parent. She tried her best to shelter me from parties and boys in particular. My mom knew that I was "boy crazy" and she was determined to prevent me from dating or having anything to do with boys.

I was so excited that my mom was finally allowing me to go somewhere fun; it was going to be my first time at the Castle. I started getting ready. This was an opportunity of a lifetime for me. Knowing my mom, I thought, "this may be my first and last time going."

As I got ready, I can remember getting in the shower and talking to God. I said, "God, I want to find my boyfriend tonight. Send him my way, even if I'm not ready now. I don't want to wait any longer."

That night, my friend Sherry and I played a game, whoever collected the most phone numbers would win. At the end of the night I had three numbers and she had two. I had so much fun dancing and getting numbers. I thought I was all that and a bag of chips.

During this time in my life, I knew God. I had received the Holy Spirit in my life at the age of twelve. I prayed and talked to Him but I was what some call a "baby Christian." I was very immature about spiritual things. I would do things I knew were wrong and pray that my mom didn't catch me.

Low self-esteem with an open heart

One of the phone numbers I got that night was Ryan's. Ryan became my first boyfriend. Although most of our relationship was spent talking on the phone, we became very close. He told me that he "loved" me after two months of being his girlfriend and I thought I was in love. What really made me feel sorry for him was when he told me that his mother died when he was five. I felt bad for him and started liking him more.

Women with low self-esteem often have a natural tendency to nurture and cater to men who are less fortunate. It's also easier to relate to others who are hurting and struggling when you're in the same position. We attract people in our comfort zone instead of connecting with others who stretch you to be better. We are more comfortable being the smartest and the one with more stability; it helps with our insecurities.

I wanted to help him. It touched my heart to know his mom was deceased. To my understanding, the deep sympathy I felt for him was love. I thought what we were developing was true love. Ryan lived with his Dad and he didn't have a mother figure in his life. I lived with my mom and didn't have a father figure in my life. I felt like I related to him, but I also believed that I needed to help him.

Sometimes, believing you can help or change someone creates a strong foundation of commitment and a false sense of love for a person who may not be the right one for you. Ryan had a dysfunctional life and I could tell he had no relationship with God.

I felt sorry for Ryan and I grew to love him although in the beginning I was not attracted to him. As a matter of fact, I thought he was very unattractive, but he was so sweet to me and he really seemed to like me a lot. I could tell because he would call me all the time and we would talk about everything. Plus, I was desperate and void of love, so to finally have someone who really cared about me in my life was amazing.

Taken by temptation

Ryan and I talked on the phone everyday after school for six months before we saw each other again. I thought we had something special. It had been six months and we finally met again at the Castle. I almost forgot what he looked like, but when I saw him standing in the party room, I knew it was Ryan. We hugged and kissed and for the first time and I felt a strong connection.

We did not want to leave when the time came but I was so happy about seeing him that I couldn't stop talking about him the whole night with Sherry.

Ryan and I continued our "phone relationship" until one day he said, "It's been seven months since we've been together; when are we going to have sex?"

"Ryan, you know I'm a virgin and I'm not ready to have sex. I'm saving myself."

"What do you mean you're saving yourself? We're in love and we have been together for a long time. Seven months is a long time, right?"

I couldn't believe he was pressuring me; it made me furious. I liked the relationship we had; I liked the attention, the communication, and the hugs and kisses. I didn't need to have sex. I was afraid of the unknown. I was very upset so I decided to dump him.

He was heated, but when I hung the phone up in his face, he called me back immediately. I didn't answer at first, but he kept calling so I finally answered.

"What do you want; it's over?"

"Rainie, I'm sorry. I don't want to break up but we should consider having sex eventually."

I thought, "Maybe he's right, maybe I should consider having him be my first and take my virginity. It's been seven months since we have been together and we are in love." Back then, seven months seemed like a long time to me.

The next time I saw Ryan it was a month later. We met up at a park; we hugged and kissed as usual but this time it was different. I was different; all I could think about was how much I loved him and how much I wanted him to be my first. I was no longer afraid of the unknown. I thought to myself, "even if he's not the one for me, even if our relationship doesn't last, I want him to be the one I give my virginity to."

I was fed up with being "Miss Goody Two Shoes" virgin. I had no idea what I was getting myself into.

I was so busy worrying about what people thought of me and making him happy while facing my fears.

Sometimes you make life-changing decisions that aren't the best for you because of your personal insecurities and fears. This is why it's so important to evaluate yourself and the entire situation.

A few months prior, I was happy and content with being a virgin. I enjoyed my situation. I enjoyed my life. But the fear of losing someone I thought I loved caused me to pursue a plan to lose my virginity. In my mind I thought it was what I wanted, but deep down I was thinking about pleasing him and catering to his desires.

When you're broken with the mindset to do your will regardless and if it lines up with God's will, you will compromise your values. When you are desperate with low self-esteem, you are willing to deny yourself of what's best for you and you carelessly accept whatever is convenient all in the name of the deception of "false love." You are chasing something you think will fill you, but it consistently leaves you empty.

A month after losing my virginity, I was convicted by the Holy Spirit and the fear of God was all over me. It was strong; it was heavy; and I needed to change quickly or something really bad was going to happen. I began to become extremely afraid of getting pregnant or contracting an STD. I decided I didn't want to have sex with Ryan again.

I realized that I didn't enjoy having sex and there were several risks involved in continuing this kind of relationship. I had dreams of one day going to college and traveling the world, and I wasn't willing to sacrifice any of my dreams to be stuck with a baby out of wedlock. I had my issues; I was broken and desperate for love, but God gave me the confidence of having something better. God showed me I didn't have to settle for something I didn't want to do just to please someone else. My Heavenly Father covered me with forgiveness and unconditional love and I promised Him I would stop.

I told Ryan we could no longer have sex. He seemed upset and wanted to know why but I had no answer for him. There was no answer he could understand.

Love lost

I noticed our relationship changed almost immediately after I told him there would be no more pre-marital sex. Ryan stopped calling me, and when we did talk on the phone, he barely had anything to say. He became very distant towards me. One day I got fed up and broke up with him. I assumed he would do what he did in the past and call me back and beg me not to leave him, but he didn't. Instead, he didn't call me back; he let me go completely and my pride was too strong to call him back. I knew he wasn't meant to be with me, and as hard as it was, I had to let him go completely.

I was so devastated. I felt a sharp pain on the inside of my chest. I would cry every night for months. I was depressed. I told myself, "If Ryan could do this to me and he really loved me, I can never experience love."

Love hurt too badly. I stopped wanting love, I was mad at love. I began believing that since I had lost my virginity, it didn't matter if I continued to have sex because I had failed and my purity was destroyed.

I realized I had been chasing a premature blessings and I didn't care if the timing was right. I was so empty and so broken that I didn't even care if what I was pursuing or seeking was right for me. I was so desperate that I was willing to compromise the purpose and plan God had for my life with a quick temporary solution.

Instead of seeking the Lord and waiting on Him in regard to my relationship, I clung onto the first man who showed me love, attention and conversation. I was desperate and lonely.

Commitment to God

One evening at a church conference, I had a spiritual encounter with God. He used the speaker to minister to my heart. She shared her story of being promiscuous and the major effects it had on her life. That night I made a vow to God, my future husband and future children that I would abstain from sex before marriage.

God said, "I'm calling you to wait on me so that your strength will be renewed. I'm strengthening you. You will mount up with wings as eagle, soaring over the temptations of the enemy. When you wait, you will be well prepared to overcome each situation with peace." God says, "Trust me and wait."

"But they that wait upon the Lord shall renew their strength; they shall mount up with wings as eagles; they shall run, and not be weary; and they shall walk, and not faint." –Isaiah 40:31

We are in this thing called life, and we get so focused on "having" that we forget how to just "Be". God wants to do mighty and amazing things in our lives but we must stay connected to Him. What I've noticed is that we may start off following God's will, but then when the pressure becomes intense, we become anxious. Therefore we do our best to "help God" or rely on our "self help" by figuring things out on our own. We must remember to lean on God, call on Him, and trust Him when the pressure is increased so that after the fire, we will come out as pure gold.

I was rebellious to God; I didn't care if I was in His will. "For rebellion is as the sin of witchcraft, and stubbornness is as iniquity and idolatry."-1 Samuel 15:23

I was a baby Christian and God's mercy and grace covered me. He allowed me to experience a situation outside of His will, but once the lesson was learned, I had to repent and turn to Him.

In order to know God's will for your life, you need to learn how to know and recognize the voice of God. Then you question yourself, "Have I received direction, confirmation and peace with all these things I'm pursuing? Or am I doing what "I" think I need to do? There's a big difference. The most challenging part of hearing God is the fact that it takes time to learn to discern His voice -- and it takes a humble heart.

Jeremiah 29:12-13 says, "Then you will call upon Me and go and pray to Me, and I will listen to you. And you will seek Me and find Me, when you search for Me with all your heart."

The more you spend time with God praying, the more you will know His voice. It's a deep knowing inside your heart. Jesus said in John 10:27, "My sheep hear My voice, and I know them, and they follow Me." The bible teaches us to train ourselves to discern both good and evil.

"But solid food belongs to those who are of full age, that is, those who by reason of use have their senses exercised to discern both good and evil." -Hebrews 5:14

It is by practicing and becoming familiar that we are able to discern whether what we hear is of God, our flesh, or the devil.

When you get the vision of being married, you must understand that there's a season and time for everything. Habakkuk 2:3 says, "For still the vision awaits its appointed time; it hastens to the end, it will not lie. If it seems slow, wait for it; it will surely come; it will not delay."

If you're spending less time with God, becoming stressed and overwhelmed, there's a good chance you're operating outside of the will of God. With God, there's peace.

"Peace I leave with you, my peace I give unto you: not as the world gives, I give to you. Let not your heart be troubled, neither let it be afraid."-John 14:27

Remember that God gave Abram the big vision: "then He brought him outside and said, look now toward heaven, and count the stars if you are able to number them. And He said to him, so shall your descendants be"-Genesis 15:5

God promised to make Abram a father. He would be blessed with a child and his descendants would be too many to count them all. But Abram and his wife Sarai tried to "help" God and "manifest" the vision on their own instead of waiting for the Lord.

"Now Sarai, Abram's wife, had borne him no children. And she had an Egyptian maidservant whose name was Hagar. So Sarai said to Abram, 'See now the Lord has restrained me from bearing children. Please, go in to my maid; perhaps I shall obtain children by her.' And Abram heeded the voice of Sarai.

Then Sarai, Abram's wife, took Hagar her maid, the Egyptian, and gave her to her husband Abram to be his wife. So he went in to Hagar, and she conceived. And when she saw that she had conceived, her mistress became despised in her eyes." –Genesis 16:1-4

Sarai represents all the insecure women who are too consumed with their weaknesses and shortcomings. Instead of believing the word of the Lord and knowing that "I can do all things through Christ who strengthens me", our failures and letdowns distract us. Saria was so insecure that she was willing to allow her man to sleep with another woman.

I believe Sarai asked Abram to sleep with Hagar to test him. She was hoping he would say, "No, I refuse to sleep with your maid. I'm committed to you. God said He would bless us with a child. Let's wait on Him." She knew he wanted a child, and she loved him and wanted to make him happy, but she also wanted him for herself. She was hoping he would wait for her. Deep down inside, she believed she wasn't good enough. She thought she wasn't worth the wait.

One of the reasons why an insecure woman will allow a man to cheat is because she is waiting for him to rescue her. She wants to be rescued from not being enough. She wants a man to fight for her and take charge to do the right thing.

She will try to lead the situation but she really wants a man to step in and say, "No, we are going to wait on the Lord. I'm going to deny my flesh, ignore what I see and my current situation and trust God."

Abram came to her about a vision that seemed impossible, and she believed she could not deliver what he desired. She knew she was barren and couldn't have children. Instead of choosing to wait on the Lord and putting his faith in God, the one who gave the vision, Abram put his trust in man. So he had sex with Hagar. And when Hagar got pregnant, Sarai despised her.

Whenever we take our eyes off God and put them on man, we become disappointed. God never told Abram or Sari to have a child through Hagar. Instead of waiting on God, they both chased a premature blessing.

As I began to spend more time with God, seeking Him and knowing Him, I began the process of discovering myself. I learned about me and what was really best for me. God revealed my worth and value as His child.

God had a plan for me and I had work to do.

CHAPTER 2

LOOKING FOR DADDY

Pride wouldn't allow me to hurt. I was in denial of the pain I felt from not having my Father in my life.

After reading the book, "The Five Love Languages," by Gary Chapman, I discovered my primary love language is "quality time". I feel loved most when I'm spending quality time with a loved one. However, my Dad was in and out of prison from the time I was five years old to the time I graduated from college. I didn't receive any quality time from him; therefore there was a tremendous scarcity of love. I lacked love from the most important man in my life. It became normal for me to go throughout life without my father's presence and love. Whenever I spoke to him, he would tell me he loved me. But it was still not the same as experiencing a relationship with him. I began to believe I didn't need love from a man. I thought I could experience a wonderful life and survive without it.

Instead of having a desperate need for and void of love, I embraced a spirit of pride and control. I told myself I didn't need my Dad and I proved it with success. I accomplished educational and career goals despite the fact that I was a fatherless child. I replaced my sad thoughts of not having him with arrogant thoughts that I didn't need him. I assumed he had no impact on my life. But I was only deceiving myself; the truth is, his absence had a major impact on my life.

Ms. Independent

My Dad's absence empowered me to become Ms. Independent. His absence taught me to never need, chase after, or become desperate for a man.

Ms. Independent is a counterfeit; she is the biggest liar ever. She deceives herself and everyone she comes in contact with. She believes and lives her lie; she says, "I don't need a man, I can be bad all by myself. I'm going to be successful, talented and spiritual, and

I don't need anyone to do it." But really, it's all an illusion; she wears a mask and disguises herself from the truth. The truth is that Ms. Independent is broken, afraid and very needy. She is desperate for love. She feeds off all the love she can get; and when she senses any evidence of love lacking, she uses the spirit of pride to control and manipulate in order to gain more love. This is her power. It's important to her to stay strong; she hates being vulnerable and looking weak. Ms. Independent has to keep it together. She has a role and position to live up to. She's led by fear; she's afraid of being alone. Even when she's in a relationship with a good man, she unconsciously pushes him away. Discontent and scarcity of love can interfere in the relationship and push genuine love away.

What if you push him too far so that he leaves? Then your pride won't allow you to pursue him. Your pride will let him go. This is one of the reasons over 50% of marriages end in divorce. People are practicing divorce before they get married. Not many are humble enough to pursue true love, such as the love of the bible.

"Love is patience, love is kind, love does not envy, love does not parade itself, is not puffed up; does not behave rudely, does not rejoice in iniquity, but rejoices in the truth; bears all things, believes all things, hopes all things, endures all things. (1 Corinthians 13:4-7)

When God blesses you with a good man, instead of complaining about what he's lacking (because no man is perfect), and blaming him for not being able to fulfill your big empty void, go to him with love and seek God for what's missing. Only God can fill that void. It's difficult to be Ms. Independent while having a loving relationship in preparation for marriage. When you are dating a man in preparation for marriage, there should be a partnership between you and that man. The two of you should be working towards a common vision.

The Thirstiest Woman of the Bible

You may have heard the term "thirsty" used to describe a desperate, needy woman seeking a man. A thirsty woman may have a good heart, sweet personality, and a great job, but she lacks stability in relationships.

Instead of allowing her heart to completely heal after a breakup, she'll run to the next available man. Her scarcity of love provokes her to seek love from all the wrong men. She is thirsty for love, thirsty for affection, and most of all thirsty for a man. She says, "I wouldn't thirst any more if only I had Mr. Right."

There's a woman in the bible who was known for being thirsty. Her name and age isn't revealed, but she's often referred to as "the woman at the well" or "the Samaritan woman." She had five ex-husbands and the man she was living with wouldn't commit and marry her. People looked down on her because of her lifestyle and she was known to be an outcast in her community. This was evidenced by the fact that she came to the well alone; and back in biblical times, drawing water and chatting at the well was the social highpoint of a woman's day.

Although she was disgraced in her town and didn't feel valuable, Jesus was waiting at the well to have a conversation with her.

She was shocked when Jesus asked her for a drink of water, Jews didn't speak to Samaritans and men usually didn't speak to women without their husbands present. Jesus' response to her was, "If you knew the gift of God, and who it is that is saying to you, give me a drink, you would have asked him, and he would have given you living water." (John 4:10)

Just like the woman at the well, there are women who are trying to quench a spiritual thirst with a temporal fix. This woman doesn't realize that a spiritual void is driving her to a well of men. No matter how much she draws from that well and drinks of it, she can never quench her thirst. It always leaves her feeling empty, so she find herself coming back drawing for more.

Then Jesus said to her, "Everyone who drinks of this water will be thirsty again, but whoever drinks of the water that I will give him will never be thirsty again. The water that I will give him will become in him a spring of water welling up to eternal life." (John 4:13-14) Only Jesus can quench your spiritual thirst. He said you shall thirst no more when you drink of the water I give.

Unfortunately, there are so many women thirsty today. Many of them don't know the gift of God and how to receive the living water from Jesus. Instead, they fall into the temptations and lusts of this world. Such a woman is willing to have sex with multiple men; her body becomes a sex object, functioning as a man's erotic toy. She has no clue how to surrender her life to Christ and live a holy and acceptable life.

She is broken and desperate and so distracted by what she sees, feels, and audibly hears that she neglects the spiritual side of life which is invisible, quiet and only felt and experienced through worship and prayer.

Have you ever been so thirsty that you started drinking everything you could find and nothing would quench your thirst? You tried drinking juice, tea, soda and water, but nothing could satisfy that thirst. This is exactly what we deal with on a spiritual level. When you're spiritually thirsty, you may look for any and everything to quench that thirst. You may try drugs, alcohol, food, sex, and shopping, but you can never quench that spiritual thirst with all the temporal things.

Instead of blaming your absent father, abusive mother or that loved one who abandoned you, offer your brokenness and empty heart to God. Jesus said,

"But the hour is coming, and is now here, when the true worshipers will worship the Father in spirit and truth, for the Father is seeking such people to worship him. God is spirit, and those who worship him must worship in spirit and truth." (John 4:23-24)

It would be years before I would come to understand and apply the "love" from the bible to my life. My Dad wrote me several letters while he was in prison. I read and cherished them as I received them, but I never wrote back. I thought about writing back but I didn't. I can recall my mom telling me that I was the child and I didn't need to worry about writing him.

I began to believe that since he was my dad and he wasn't there, he owed me and I didn't have to give back to anyone who owe me. I was holding on to resentment and pain. I couldn't forgive and love him without feeling upset; I was often reminded of the scarcity of his love. This taught me to be open and willing to receive from a man but never feel obligated to give anything. I applied this thinking to every relationship. I could never be the one asking a man on a date; and if I were dating someone and he made me mad, I would quickly dump him. I wouldn't allow myself to be in a situation were I was being dumped. I had to be in control.

Ms. Control

Ms. Control convinces herself that the world around her will fall a part if she's not in control. She often tries to figure out how she can manipulate and spin situations to her advantage. She can get very upset when things don't go her way. Although she can use her alluring appearance and sex appeal to capture a man, she struggles to keep him. Her controlling spirit can be aggressive and possessive, often sending a man away. She honestly believes nothing good can happen without her input, without her direction, and without her control. She believes her way is the only true way to go. She is very self-centered.

Ladies, it's important to understand that you can't control anyone but yourself. When a man doesn't treat you kindly and love you the way you desire, pay attention to what he's showing you. Instead of trying to manipulate the situation to make him chose you, let him be. Don't sabotage yourself by using your power of control to get him to do what you want; the relationship won't last and it will only be devastating for you in the end. We are very powerful, and most women know exactly what they need to do to get a man's attention. It doesn't take rocket science, but very few women know how to capture his heart. Capturing a man's heart requires so much more than having a beautiful figure and wearing tight clothes. One of the things it requires is for a woman to let go completely of all temporal things and embrace the eternal. You must be willing to surrender and trust that your spirit and soul alone are enough to attract true lasting love.

When you're not careful enough to pay attention to the people you are attracting, you can easily attract "the predator."

The Predator

Have you been attracting predators in your life? The predator is a man who actively and aggressively preys on weak and broken women. He comes in all heights, weights, and various ethnic groups. He can be worldly, spiritual, religious or agnostic. He is always hunting for a woman, but not just any woman; he wants a special women. He wants a woman with low self-esteem who lacks confidence. He wants a woman who is desperate and thirsty for a man. If she's broken, confused and needy, she's perfect for the predator. He will use all his schemes and tactics to get her hooked. Once he knows she's hooked, he will use her up until there's nothing left. He will use her for whatever she can offer: sex, money, shelter, ego boost, quality time, power, and even control.

The predator is the modern wolf in sheep's clothing. His initial introduction is very appealing to a woman. He may appear to be attractive, kind, helpful and mesmerizing, but in reality he has an agenda to get what he came for and move on.

Sadly, women welcome predators in their lives every day. These predators become fathers to their children, stay-at-home boyfriends, and they even become husbands. Predators feed off weak women because they are weak insecure men. These men are fascinated with appearing to have the good life; they want to look good, gain lots of respect, and live life on their terms only. They are self-centered and very arrogant. The bible warns of them. It says, "They are the kind who worm their way into homes and gain control over gullible women, who are loaded down with sins and are swayed by all kinds of evil desire, always learning but never able to come to a knowledge of truth." (2 Timothy 3:6-7)

Men who cheat are often praised and acknowledged as players, pimps, and sometimes aspiring male role models for some young boys.

Any man can cheat, but it takes a strong man to be faithful. This is why it's so important to not wait until after you fall in love with a man to ask God, "is he's the one for me." Instead, you need to ask God in the very beginning if he is the one.

CHAPTER 3

WINNING IN THE DATING GAME

I went from being lonely, empty and desperate for a man to becoming heart broken, hopeless and resentful towards being in a relationship. I didn't want love; I guarded my heart to the point that no one could come in. I had built an invisible wall to protect my heart.

I was determined to never allow someone else to hurt me again. In my mind, "all men were dogs" and "real love didn't exist." I didn't trust men but I was still willing to "hang out" or "just have fun"--nothing serious.

Still Playing the Dating Game

I was playing the dating game, but this time I was determined to protect myself. Who was I kidding?

I was weak and vulnerable but tried my best to not get hurt. It's like playing with fire. You may practice a few tricks to keep from getting burned, but there's a huge chance the fire will catch hold of you.

During this season, I "talked" to several guys. When I say we were "talking", I mean we spent time together, and sometimes cuddled and kissed. But there was no sex involved and I would not allow myself to get serious with anyone. Plus, I made a vow and a commitment to God and my future husband and children and I would not go against it.

Players will play

I met Mr. Player. He thought he was God's gift to women. He thought he was the finest man on the planet. In the beginning I didn't know he was a serial cheater so I was open to developing a dating relationship with him. He was charming and knew how to make me smile, but I learned very quickly; he was this way with several girls. I would find out he was dating someone's cousin and another girl's friend, and another friend's sister. It was so bad that I found myself despising the "other girl" instead of getting rid of him.

For the first time in my life I started comparing myself to other women. What does she have that I don't have? Why can't he just be faithful to me? What's wrong with me?

I knew something had to change fast because I didn't like how insecure I was becoming. After finding out about a recent girlfriend, I was fed up. He told me he liked us both and it was hard to choose.

Too Guarded to Get Hurt

When you're involved in the "dating world" and there's no purpose and direction, you can easily fall into dysfunctional situations. You may question, how did I get here? How did I end up in a relationship with a man who is a habitual cheater? How did I become a jealous insecure woman who despises other women I don't even know? The great thing about this relationship was the fact that I was too guarded to get hurt. I would never have sex with him and I never opened my heart to fully trust him.

"Guard your heart with all diligence, for from it flows the springs of life." –Proverbs 4:23

But still I was idle. When you date, you should always have a purpose in mind. You should know the type of relationship God is leading you to. I call it spiritual dating. This is dating that is spiritually led. Prayer is very heavily involved as well as spiritual meditation and guidance of the Holy Spirit. Unfortunately, I had no direction; plus I was involved in this meaningless relationship. He told me he wanted her and me. I told him that this was impossible and I would never allow it, so instead of waiting on him to pick her or chose me, I made the decision to leave him.

I wasn't fully committed to anyone. I had other guy friends. They were friends whom I enjoyed talking to, laughing with, and hanging out. Although I was dating men I was attracted to, I remained guarded and determined not to give too much of myself. This was my protection. This is what kept me safe from the devastation of being taken advantage of by a predator and experiencing the pain of a broken heart.

Looks are deceiving

Then I met "Pretty Boy". He was very funny; he could always make me laugh. He was also very handsome and tall. There were several girls who wanted to be with him but he definitely didn't take anyone too seriously. I thought he was fun to be around.

During this time, I was a senior in high school and this was before social media, a time when people actually spent hours talking on the phone. There was no hiding behind a text message or finding out how your day was going by checking Facebook or Twitter. We had conversations. We talked about music and movies; we talked about how we felt about each other. I knew Pretty Boy was sexually active and he assumed I was a virgin because I told him I was not sexually active. We didn't pursue anything serious but we both enjoyed each other's company. There was something about him, something that lured me towards him.

One day after talking on the phone with Pretty Boy, he decided to click over and add his friend to the conversation. He called his friend, Patrick. I had heard about Patrick before but I had never met him or even had a conversation with him. Pretty Boy and Patrick were good friends and they would rap together. For some reason they thought they were musically talented. Pretty Boy had lots of people calling him. He kept getting other phone calls and he would click over and leave Patrick and me on hold while he talked to whoever was calling. It was very awkward at first because I didn't know Patrick that well but we would make conversation. While I talked to Patrick, I was worried about whom Pretty Boy was talking to and what was taking so long. Finally he clicked back onto the line with Patrick and me, and said, "I'm going to have to call you two later."

I said, "If you get off the phone with me, I'm going to give Patrick my number because we are having a good conversation and now you're making us get off the phone just because you have another call."

Failing the test

I wanted to make Pretty Boy jealous in hopes that he wouldn't get off the phone with me. I thought I could control him with the threat of getting closer to his friend. Just like the story I shared in Chapter 1, Sarai tested Abram and now I was testing Pretty Boy. I wanted to test how much he liked me and wanted to be with me. Unfortunately he failed the test. He didn't care. It didn't bother him that I would talk to his friend without him being present. So I said, "Give me a call, Patrick." And I gave Patrick my number.

Then Pretty Boy said, I'll talk to you later."

I didn't really want to talk to Patrick; I was just trying to make his friend jealous, but Patrick called me right back immediately. We actually had a good conversation. I talked to him about the guys I was dating; he talked to me about the girls he dated. He gave me advice from a male perspective and I shared wisdom from a female point of view. I found it very refreshing to be open and honest about my life with a man I had no interest in dating. Patrick became a good friend. We started talking often. He was a great listener; I didn't realize how much I needed someone to listen to me.

The word of the Lord

Then came Mr. "Man of God" (according to what he expressed to me on good days). He was attractive and talented, plus he was one of the first guys my mom liked. She thought he was cute. I would see him often at church and he attended my sweet 16 birthday party.

He had wanted to date me for over a year and I finally gave him a chance. I enjoyed our friendship and quality time together. He started to become important to me. My heart had softened towards him because he made me feel special. He and I became close, but he knew in the very beginning of our relationship that I was not sexually active and was planning to save myself for marriage. He didn't have a problem with that; as a matter of fact he told me God told him I was going to be his wife. Immediately after he said these words I thought, "God didn't tell me that." I had a relationship with God and I knew what he was telling me was not the truth.

"My sheep hear My voice, and I know them, and they follow Me." - John 10:27

I continued the relationship. I really cared about him and was hopeful for our future although I didn't know where it would lead me.

I stood on my vow; I stood on the promise I made to God and my future husband and children. But the enemy will always come with temptation. He will try to tempt you to sin against God.

"No temptation has seized you except what is common to a man. And God is faithful; he will not let you be tempted beyond what you can bear. But when you are tempted, he will also provide a way out so that you can stand up under it." -1 Corinthians 10:13

The enemy thought that if he could deceive me into believing that Mr. "Man of God" was my husband, I would give in and have sex with him. Although I really liked Mr. Man of God, I continued to have friendships with other men.

Patrick and I had become best friends, and at times I would call him my "Play Brother". However, I noticed I hadn't spoken with him in a while. It had been at least two weeks so I decided to give him a call.

"Hey stranger, where have you been? I missed talking to you. It's been a while."

"I decided to give you your space since you have a boyfriend now. You were very happy about Mr. Man of God so I decided to step back."

"If you're my friend, why should it bother you if I'm dating someone?"

I could tell Patrick was starting to have feelings

for me even though he didn't verbally address it. I enjoyed our friendship and I really liked having a male friend who would listen and share advice, but he was my friend and nothing more, nothing less. I was a little upset that he purposely stopped calling me because I was dating Mr. Man of God. Although I liked Mr. Man of God, I didn't want to lose a friend like Patrick over him.

Rejection once again

One night I received a phone call from Mr. Man of God. I could tell by the tone of his voice that something wasn't right.

"Rainie, I need to talk to you about something that's very important to me."

"Sure let's talk."

"I've been with you for a while now and I'm very frustrated because we don't see each other enough, and I'm used to being sexually active with my lady. And you are not willing to give yourself to me in that way, so I'm going to have to break up with you."

I was devastated. I was hurt and very disappointed. This man told me that God told him I was going to be his wife; he told me I was the one, and that he loved me and was willing to wait for me. How could he leave me that easily with no remorse? I was shocked; I did not expect this. I had heard rumors that there was another woman in his life and she was spending a lot of time with him. But all I could think about was, "here I am again, rejected by another man. I guess no man is willing to wait for me. I made this promise to God but it feels like a curse. How can I expect to be loved and accepted unconditionally if every man wants sex before marriage?"

I could feel the tears rolling down my face as I got off the phone. This was my very last conversation with the so-called Mr. Man of God. I felt so low, so down and out. I thought I would be rewarded for being determined to live for God; instead it felt like a punishment.

Be encouraged

Ten minutes after I got off the phone with Mr. Man of God, the phone rang. It was my friend Patrick. I told him I was no longer dating Mr. Man of God and he dumped me because I refused to have sex with him.

Patrick listened to me talk and then spoke, "If that's the reason he dumped you, then he doesn't deserve to have you. You are worth so much more than that."

It was the sweetest thing I'd ever heard a man say to me. His words gave me so much life at that moment. Although I was sad, I gained some hope from hearing those words. God used Patrick to encourage me that night. I felt like God was saying, "Rainie, don't give up; there's hope; you are not alone."

That night I cried while lying in my bed. I was fed up with the "dating culture". I resigned from the "dating game". I was done. I thought about the heartbreak I felt from Ryan, the insecurity of being with Mr. Player, the disappointment of Mr. Pretty Boy, and the rejection of Mr. Man of God--all of them were predators. They all preyed on my weakness; they all tried to use me for something and I'd had enough. I was done. I no longer wanted anything to do with dating. All I could do was cry out to God. "Lord, I'm so tired of being lied to, cheated on, rejected and used. I no longer want a boyfriend. I don't want to date ever again. God send me my husband, I want to wait on the man you would have for me to marry. I'm done playing these games. I'm tired of worrying about whether or not a man will love me for me and sick of doing things to make a man happy while denying my happiness. God, I want your best. I want what you are preparing for me."

This was one of the most powerful prayers I've ever prayed and I meant every word. I meant it from the bottom of my heart. God knew I was serious this time; he knew I was ready. "The righteous cry, and the Lord hears, and delivers them out of all their troubles." –Psalms 34:17

I had finally decided to surrender it all to God. I surrendered wanting to be loved/ I surrendered wanting to be in a committed relationship and I surrendered the feelings of rejection and disappointment. There comes a time when things aren't going the way you would like them to. You may not have the man you've been hoping and praying for, or maybe you have a man but his heart is not completely committed to you. There are conditions to his love and God is calling you to end the relationship, but you are struggling with letting go. You may be holding onto a relationship you want to be right, but it's just not right; it's not of God and you're trying to bless it and make it Godly.

"Surrender your heart to God, turn to him in prayer, and give up your sins — even those you do in secret. Then you won't be ashamed; you will be confident and fearless." -Job 11:13-15

God is calling you to surrender to Him completely. Release the pressures and weight of trying to make an ungodly relationship work when it's not meant to be. Give the entire situation to God and allow Him to minister to your heart during the brokenness. You may feel like a failure because you're not married or you're in love with a man who uses you, but God can heal your broken heart. All you have to do is surrender it all to Jesus.

CHAPTER 4

❖

GETTING OVER A BREAK UP

When God has a calling on your life, there are times when He will separate you from people, places and things. He will call you out and set you apart. When God isolates you, He is bringing you closer to Him and He will remove all the distractions in your life.

Breaking up with "Mr. Wrong" is necessary because it prepares you for a greater level in life and it sets you up to receive Mr. Right. I often hear women say, "I'm currently dating this guy but I know he's not right for me. I just don't know how to end it." You must first be willing to let go in order to receive what's best for you.

During this particular season of separation in my life, I surrendered my need to "have" a man and became more content and satisfied with my life as a single woman. I learned how to enjoy my own company; I became comfortable with being by myself and I was at peace with not being in a relationship.

You must first become comfortable listening to your thoughts, writing down your ideas and visions, and loving you without a man. I started to enjoy my quiet time meditating, praying and reading. My time was focused on personal development; reading, exercising and painting are still some of my favorite hobbies.

I stopped coveting a man and started delighting myself in God. My relationship with the Lord deepened and the desires of my heart changed. Breaking up with Mr. Wrong may feel scary at first and heart breaking, but it's the best thing you can do for yourself. Toxic people will block new opportunities and blessing in your life.

I remember having a very negative friend years ago; she was very toxic and confrontational. She was always in some type of drama and always mad at someone. She and I ended our friendship because of some drama she started, and I notice a few months after ending my friendship with her just how peaceful and stress-free my life became. You may feel sad in the beginning of a break up, but after a while you'll realize that it's best for you.

Loving Me and Dreaming Big

I started working on my purpose instead of pursuing a person. I made plans to travel the world, leave St. Louis and go to college in a bigger city. I planned to study fashion design and art. I had goals I wanted to accomplish, and being in a relationship was no longer at the top of my priority list.

I can relate to Abram's message from God in Genesis 12:1-3: "Now the Lord said to Abram, go from your country and your kindred and your father's house to the land that I will show you. And I will make of you a great nation, and I will bless you and make your name great, so that you will be a blessing. I will bless those who bless you, and him who dishonors you I will curse, and in you all the families of the earth shall be blessed."

God revealed the calling on my life. He showed me that He had a purpose for me. I wasn't to just go anywhere and date just anyone, but God had a specific plan and purpose for me and I was supposed to wait on the Lord.

It's very important that you do not become careless. It's easy for a woman with a broken heart to become bitter and resentful towards men. You can easily become cold hearted and spiteful. It's important that you understand that there's a reason your past relationship did not last; there's a reason you didn't have any peace. God has a specific purpose for your life. If you will let go and surrender the need to be in control, He will direct your path and show you exactly what to do.

"The steps of a good man are ordered by the Lord: and he delights in his way." –Psalms 37: 23

No matter how difficult things may become, it's important that you put your trust in God and not in the current situation. Don't get distracted by the way things look around you. The reason consecration is so important is because when you remove negative things out of your life, you can clearly see and easily receive what God is doing. When your relationships consist of the wrong people, and you are engaged in the wrong situations, you can unintentionally block your blessings.

The Strength of a Good Friend

As I embraced my new season of consecration, most of my time was spent going to school and working. I wasn't involved in a relationship, but my friendship with Patrick began to strengthen.

Patrick and I would talk often on the phone and sometimes he would drive me to work. I could rely on him. I didn't have a vehicle and he did and his support meant so much to me. Not only was he a good friend to me, but I was a committed friend to him, cared for him and valued his friendship above other so-called friends.

I noticed that I felt safe and free around Patrick. I could freely share private information that I was too ashamed to share with others. I talked to him about my father being in prison and how it made me feel, and he also shared insight about his father's past addiction and disability. We would also talk about our future goals and plans.

Patrick was an athlete. He played both baseball and football and would invite me to his games. One night after leaving his football game, I was so hungry.

We stopped at a restaurant to pick up some tacos, and I immediately started eating them in the car. In the past, I would normally eat slowly and neatly when a male was around; I was usually very careful about the way I ate. But I noticed when I was with Patrick, it was like being with my buddy or someone I had known all my life. I ate those tacos as if I were sitting at the dinner table with my family. I didn't care if I had sauce on my face or if I stuffed my mouth. I felt so free and very comfortable around Patrick.

Our friendship was enhanced more and more and on Christmas day, Patrick called me and said, "Merry Christmas, are you busy right now?"

"No, I'm not busy, what's up?"

"I have something I want to give you. Can I stop by?"

"Sure, you can come by."

Patrick came by my house to give me a card. The card said, "Your friendship means the world to me and I enjoy each moment we share. No matter where life leads us, you will always have a special place in my heart. Merry Christmas!"

After reading the card, I looked up and noticed him watching me. It was so sweet; it was such a special card. I was thankful and surprised to get such a heartfelt card from him. I also felt sorry because I didn't have a gift for him, although he didn't expect one; he just wanted to express his appreciation of our friendship. He asked if I would be interested in going to the movies with him that evening. I didn't have any plans and didn't want to sit in the house all day watching TV, so I decided to go. This was new; I had never been to the movies on Christmas day.

I didn't view it as a date. We were buddies and we had fun together. But this night seemed special; it was unique. As we sat side-by-side in the movie theater, I felt a strong urge to hold his hand and so I did. We held hands and I felt a sweet connection--a genuine sentimental moment. I thought about how much I really enjoyed his company. I thought about how safe I felt when he was around. Everything in that moment felt right. I was with my friend and it was an amazing moment.

Misery Loves Company

Unfortunately, the happy feelings I felt in that moment would soon end. The movie was over and we walked out of the theater holding hands. While we were walking to the car, approaching us was none other than Mr. Player with a confused looked on his face. He called my name and asked why I was there with Patrick. I told him that Patrick was my friend and kept walking. I could tell Mr. Player was upset and disappointed. I was shocked to see him and confused by his reaction at seeing me with Patrick.

How could he be upset when I hadn't spoken to him in months? We were over and done. What did he expect? Did he think I would sit around and wait for him to call me? Did he think he was irreplaceable?

I was so perplexed. I went from feeling such a sweet connection with my dear friend Patrick to feeling confused and uncertain about my feelings of anxiety and alarm towards Mr. Player. I had been doing fine before I bumped into him. Suddenly, old feelings and indecisive emotions consumed me.

For the rest of the night all I could think about was Mr. Player's reaction to seeing me with Patrick. It ruined the remainder of the evening and I was ready to go home. Mr. Player called me the next day.

"Why were you with that dude, holding hands leaving the movie theater?"

"We are friends and we decided to go to the movies. Why should it matter? You and I are no longer together."

"I just couldn't believe you would be out with someone other than me."

I could tell Mr. Player was hurt. Although he cheated and dated another girl while he was with me, he never expected to see me out with someone else. We both knew that we could never be together again and this was the last conversation I had with Mr. Player.

Desperate For Love

I realized in that moment that Mr. Player wasn't hurt because he wanted to be with me, but he was hurt because I had finally moved on without him in my life. Predators cheat because of their own insecurities. They prey off broken individuals who are desperate for love. My hunger and need for love allowed him to cheat and be the player in our relationship. The cheating had nothing to do with me. I was good enough and I deserved better. I've learned to never allow myself to be desperate for a person's love. Only God can fill you up with an abundance of love; God is love.

Whenever you are desperate for the love, attention and the approval of people, you become vulnerable to users. Users have one purpose: to get what they want from you and leave when it's convenient.

A Letter to Users

Thanks for being you and showing me your purpose in my life. You were meant to open my eyes to the reality of true snakes. You often appear to be friendly, spiritual and insightful when all along you were using me. You got close enough to discover my gifts and be in the midst of my creativity; and when you felt you could do the same, you left. I wish you much success in that. I release you and no longer allow you to be apart of my life and my circle. Thanks for teaching me a great lesson. Oh, and by the way, I forgive you!

Users come in all income levels, nationalities, genders and ethnic groups. They are all around. Anytime they have an opportunity to benefit from using you, they will.

A letter to Impostors

Dear Impostor, I didn't deal with you much in the beginning, but later you won me over. You pretended to love me and support me, and I thought you liked me, but all along you were trying to replace me. When it was exposed, you tried to blame me as if it were my fault. I was too naive to see what you were doing. I was too busy suppressing the conflict and covering the deceit with busy work. My eyes are wide open now and I see you for who you really are. You showed me something great; you showed me how wonderful I am and how much I'm needed, envied and desired.

A Letter to Jealousy

Dear Jealousy, You amaze me because while your life appears to be blessed, you can't keep your eyes off my blessings. I observed you studying me and comparing what I had. You explored what I was doing in order to improve your life. You've been a snake from the start. You allowed your ego to control the situations between us, and you used me. I gave you a platform to help you grow and when you did, you distanced yourself from me. Your envy is obvious. You taught me to analyze the signs of a person. Pay attention to the details, write out everything, and judge the fruit of their soul.

A Letter to Spectator

I forgive you for noticing me, seeing my gifts and judging me from afar. You never tried to get to know the real me; instead you disregarded me which led me to question myself and whether or not I was good enough. It pushed me to work harder and try to be more when all along I was enough, and I am enough. I'm not sure what you wanted, expected or believed about me, but at this point in my life, it doesn't matter. I'm at peace with being me. You taught me that everything is not for me. One day you'll realize that you missed out. I won't be available for you. I surrender to God fully and bless you from afar.

The Blessing of Forgiveness

Once I forgave all the users in my life, I flowed on a level of peace and contentment that surpassed all understanding. There I was in that moment, season and time, happier than I've ever been. I was so grateful and blessed to experience wholeness without needing a man. I was validated in Christ. I was gifted of a deep relationship with God. I lacked no good thing. I knew I was blessed and everywhere I went, everyone I encountered saw my blessings. When the Holy Spirit lives in you, there's no denying the strong presence and alluring power of God that attracts others to you. It's a spiritual encounter and awakening. There is a confidence and upright demeanor about you.

The One for Him

The more Patrick and I spent time together, the more his feelings for me were undeniable. Patrick told me he loved me and I was shocked.

"How do you know you love me? We're just great friends, right?"

"I've been knowing I love you for a while now."

"Well thanks for letting me know."

"Would you be my girlfriend?"

"That's flattering, Patrick, but I like our friendship… lets keep it that way."

I wasn't ready for a relationship and especially not with my good friend. I valued our friendship so much and I didn't want to ruin it, plus I only saw him as a friend. Patrick had finally confirmed that he had feelings for me. Although I could tell, this was the first time he verbally communicated his love for me.

I thought he was a sweetheart and I wanted the best for him, so that night I prayed that God would send Patrick the right girl. I prayed that she would have a loving genuine spirit. That she wouldn't be a user or a cheater but would have a pure loving heart towards him. I wanted my friend to be happy but I was convinced I wasn't the one for him.

CHAPTER 5

❖

THE MATCH MADE IN HEAVEN

Waiting on God is a process. It's a daily dependency on the guidance of the Holy Spirit, a discipline that requires death to the self. My life no longer consisted of what I wanted; it was now focused on what God created me for, living my purpose and doing what God wanted me to do.

"I am crucified with Christ: nevertheless I live; yet not I, but Christ lives in me: and the life which I now live in the flesh I live by the faith of the Son of God, who loved me, and gave himself for me." – Galatians 2:20

I had to deny myself all the things I thought I should have and what I thought my life should be. I had to be willing to let go of my selfish desires and humble myself to the desires of God.

"For whosoever will save his life shall lose it; but whosoever shall lose his life for my sake and the gospel's, the same shall save it." –Mark 8:35

The Ultimate Matchmaker

Losing your life is to fully surrender it all to God. It's letting go of what I think I should do and releasing it to what God wants to do in me and through me. I had to become like clay and allow God to form and mold me into a vessel He could use. My thinking changed. If God created me for a purpose, there were specific things He would have me do, specific places for me to go, and specific people He wants me to encounter and know.

Therefore, why should I be in control of whom I date and marry? It's not up to me to find a man; it's not my purpose to chase love or beg to be wanted. God had a specific man for me.

So many single women make the same mistake I made by trying to find a man. We think we know what's best, but we don't. While you're looking at the outer appearance of that man, God knows what is inside his heart.

God sees that man twenty years from now and you are only looking at what he looks like now. He knows that man's temper and how he deals with stress. God sees that man's generational bloodline and the many mental and physical issues that occur from generation to generation.

You looking at how sweet he is toward you during your date and how thoughtful his phone calls and text messages are. You attach your heart to a man you think you know, but God knows the unseen hidden things of a man's heart. While your heart is focused on marrying someone tall, dark, and handsome, God is focused on your spiritual compatibility. Are you equally connected on a spiritual level? When the trials of life come, will the two of you survive? These are the questions only God can answer.

You must remember that God is the creator of marriage. He knows exactly what it takes to have a successful union. It's so obvious that God is the ultimate matchmaker. Why do we look to people when it comes to finding love? I decided I was putting the complications of love in God's hands. I was determined to allow God to be my personal matchmaker.

Discovering Love

One day at school, my friend Angie and I began talking about our weekend. She asked me about Patrick, and immediately I was aware something amazing happened. I had a supernatural awakening and ah ha moment, Angie's words were no longer audibly heard or comprehended.

While she was talking, an overwhelming feeling of love covered me from the inside out; and at that moment, all I could think about was how much I really loved Patrick. I had never experienced that feeling all at once before.

It was a deep knowing and assurance. "Wow, I love Patrick". The love I felt for Patrick made me excited and happy, I couldn't wait to tell him.

I realized that once I surrendered my heart fully to God and released my need to be in control, I could now love freely. Up to this point in my life, I had been selfish and focused on what I wanted only. I thought we could only have a buddy friendship kind of love and nothing more.

Now God could lead me and soften my heart to love deeply. Not only did I love Patrick, but I was also in love with him. He had become my best friend and I had a deep love for him. The love I had for him was stronger than any love once felt for Ryan, Mr. Player, or any other man I had dated.

Later that day, Patrick came by my house to visit and that's when I told him.

"I have something I would like to tell you. I really value our friendship and I want you to know I love you, but not just as a friend. I'm in love with you.

Patrick looked as if he had been waiting to hear those words for a very long time; and like a gentleman, he had been patiently waiting for this moment.

"I love you, too, and feel the same way about you. I've been in love with you and I imagine us being together for a long time. Rainie, can I have a hug?"

We hugged, and in that moment I felt a strong spiritual presence. It felt like God's confirmation; it was like a sign. I had never felt a presence like this before, especially during a hug. As he held me and I held him, I could hear the voice of God. It wasn't an audible voice; it was a soft inner voice from the heart that said, "This is your husband."

I didn't expect to receive such a prophetic word,

but in that peaceful moment, I knew one day Patrick would become my husband. I felt a peace that surpassed all understanding. The peace of God rested on the both of us in that moment. I didn't tell Patrick about the prophetic word I heard; I believe the Lord should reveal it to a man in due season at the right time.

I realized when God sent my husband, he sent him as a friend and companion who added value and support in my life. Although he wasn't my husband yet, after receiving the confirmation from God, I believed one day he would be. I thought about when God used Patrick to encourage me after being heartbroken by Mr. Man of God, who dumped me because I refused to have sex with him.

Patrick listened to me talk and then said, "If that's the reason he dumped you, then he doesn't deserve to have you. You are worth so much more than that."

I thought about all the times Patrick was there for me, how he would listen and give me advice. He was a true friend and God was doing something new and amazing in my life.

Sometimes while you're looking so hard and struggling to find love, it is right there waiting. Love is right under your nose, but it's impossible to find even if it's staring you in the face. It's our opinionated mindset and our headstrong stubborn ways that distract us from recognizing and receiving love. It takes a divine revelation an inspiration from God to know real love when it's there. It takes a willingness to let go, humble yourself, and allow God to make the love connection.

As I look back on this situation, I didn't really understand the magnitude of what had happened. In that moment, I believed in the love I had for Patrick and his love for me, but I slightly doubted we would get married one day. I was seventeen years old when God revealed this to me. Marriage was far from my mind. One thing was for sure, I really wanted to be loved and experience a loving relationship.

Marriage a calling or a craving

When God has a plan for your future, He will often start by planting a tiny seed. Many times, the promise He plants is so small and farfetched that it almost seems unbelievable. I remember about nine years ago from the day I'm writing this book that God spoke to me during my morning devotion and He told me I was going to become an entrepreneur, speaker and author.

When I first received this word, I was too afraid to write it in my journal. I was thankful but it was very difficult to believe. At that time I was working at a full-time job for a health care agency. I was over worked, stressed, overweight and fatigued. However, I received the word and wrote the vision in my journal.

As time continued to past, I watered that seed with faith. I prayed and pursued the word. I followed the guidance and direction of the Holy Spirit, and fast forward to today, I'm a full-time entrepreneur. I am the founder of a nonprofit, *Sisters of Hope*, owner of a publishing and production agency, *Rainie Howard Enterprises*, author and traveling speaker.

Therefore, at age seventeen when God planted that tiny seed revealing Patrick would be my husband, I would water that seed with faith, obedience and guidance from God. At twenty-one years of age, Patrick and I became husband and wife. Now don't get me wrong; it was a battle protecting that seed. The devil tried to steal, kill, and destroy it. Although I knew Patrick was meant to be my husband, I was not to "play house" and we were not to act like married people before our union.

The Lord made it very clear that we were not to defile our marriage by engaging in pre-marital sex, fornication, or anything else designed for a husband and wife. The temptation was strong because our love for each other was so deep, but I thank God we made it.

Is getting married your calling or craving? Some women truly have a vision of being married. They have a calling from God to embrace the role of a wife. They know because God has planted a seed. Then there are those women who are not called to be a wife but they have a craving. They crave the attention of a husband, and the beauty and glitz of a wedding. These women are more impressed with the title than the position of a wife. They don't want to be alone and they want social acceptance. Therefore, they pursue marriage with a self-centered motive. They pursue the rite to feel and look important, wanted and needed. If this is you, I want you to know that you are more than enough. Marriage will not make you happy. God will never require your fulfillment to be based on another person's involvement. Your true happiness is found in a personal relationship with God.

CHAPTER 6

❖

WHEN GOD LED ME TO MY WIFE

by Patrick Howard

Boys Becoming Men

Growing up in a single parent home as the oldest brother of two younger sisters, I had a lot of responsibilities and I matured fast because of it. I didn't have a relationship with my father, and the lack of his involvement in our home caused me to prematurely become the man of the house.

This put me in position to gain some of the responsibilities that are normally reserved for the father, but, fortunately, this experience helped me to mature quickly and provided me with insight on how to communicate with females. It also created a passion to pursue a future family free from the mistakes I had previously observed.

My goal was to create a family and life filled with joy, similar to the success of the Huxtable Family from "The Cosby Show" which was the most successful TV family I knew. I had seen so many examples of what not to do; I was sure that my experience and personality gave me a better outlook on life and insight on how to create the life I desired.

The problem with this was that I had not yet completely committed my life to Christ, so the idea that my desires and good works would guide me to the joy I sought was misguided. This mindset is a reflection of assuming that from the desires of my own heart, I could create a God-like future for myself through my own work. I was confused in believing that good works alone bring about change, but in fact they only inspire and bring momentary motivation. The reality is that all men have character flaws, even the most well-intentioned.

This is why a man can be faithful to one female and unfaithful to another. When a man is led by his feelings and emotions, he becomes open to making bad choices. For example, consider James 1:8 which state that a double minded man is unstable in all his ways.

Double-minded actions occur when a man who is not connected with God's purpose for his life, second guesses his decision to remain faithful to his woman. That man is dealing with a character flaw; and if he puts his faith in his works instead of seeking God for strength and guidance, he is prone to sin.

When a man has the motivation and courage to pursue his sinful desire to cheat while refusing to submit unto God, he often finds himself in the hands of another woman. This can occur frequently. There are also men who do not have the ambition or guts to pursue this second guess; and as a result, they do not actively become unfaithful. The deception is in thinking that a man who hasn't actually stepped out has not cheated. But Jesus teaches, "…whoever looks at a woman with lust for her has already committed adultery with her in his heart." (Matthew 5:28)

Thus, it is important for a man to be connected to God through the Holy Spirit so that his character is prepared to remain faithful whether he is full of ambition or lacks it.

This is when true change is created in the hearts and minds of men. True change comes when a person connects with the Holy Spirit and operates under the character and authority given by God through His Word.

God intends for us to operate in the fullness of all that He has created us to be, and it requires a connection with His Holy Spirit to reach the full effect of a relationship filled with lifelong joy and favor. Nevertheless, understand that this does not mean that a man will not face any temptation.

Nevertheless, a Holy Spirit connection reaffirms that a man can be confident that the testing of his faith strengthens patience and as this patience grows, he will see himself as lacking nothing. (James 1:3-4) A good personality can be a starting point to excite personal connection, but character carries the torch to ignite the flame necessary to maneuver through the dark days that every relationship encounters.

A Young Man's View on Marriage

Proverbs 18:22 states, "He who finds a wife finds a good thing, and obtains favor from the Lord." It is a commonly quoted scripture used to encourage men of the future joys that marriage brings. However, for most young men, though they seek relationships, they have no intention of finding a wife or know what it actually means to obtain favor from the Lord as a result of marriage.

As a young man, my focus was to date an attractive female I enjoyed being with. I wanted her to have a pretty smile and a cute shape, but most importantly, a sweet spirit. Rainie had all of the above and what's more, she made me happy. I never wanted our time together to end. I could tell there was something different about her; and although I cherished the moments we shared, marriage wasn't on the forefront of my mind.

It wasn't until I connected with God and received the peace of the Holy Spirit that I gained the desire to be married and prepare to one day become Rainie's husband. I needed to first be led by God.

"Wives follow the lead of your husbands as you follow the Lord" –Ephesians 5: 22

The key to this scripture is "the husband must follow the Lord." A man isn't ready to marry and lead his family until he is ready to first follow God. It wasn't until I gave my heart to the Lord and allowed Him to become the head of my life that I became ready for marriage and ready to lead and guide my family.

Finding My Wife

Rainie and I connected as friends first, and this was vital in the foundation of our relationship. As friends we were able to talk about our dreams, future goals and visions for our lives. This is why I do not regret allowing myself to be this close to the friend zone with her.

Had I not approached her as a friend first, I might not have had as much access to getting to know Rainie's authentic vision, nor would she have had the opportunity to learn mine. An understanding of life's vision is important as it gives people an idea of the direction toward which one sees themselves headed and provides clarity as to whether or not the vision is worth pursuing together.

The Bible teaches, in Habakkuk 2:2-3, to write the vision and make it plain, so that he who reads it will run… If a woman provides her vision to a man who is not willing to run with her to accomplish it, then don't wait because it will not happen. Once your vision is in the hands of a man who is willing to run for you, then I recommend you to be willing to wait for the relationship aspect of the vision to come to pass, because although you may have to wait for it to be completely right, and it may not flow as smoothly as you would like, if you wait for it, it will surely come without delay. This is how I knew that Rainie was going to be my wife and that her affection was worth waiting for.

After meeting Rainie and talking with her on multiple occasions, we became very comfortable talking with each other. Though it was a friend-zone risk I was taking, I thought this was a good way to get to know her, and it set communication as a part of the foundation of our relationship.

The friend zone is a place most men try to stay away from when they meet attractive females because there is the conception that once a man has reached it with a female, she will never desire to be in a relationship with him.

As a result, a man may try to avoid going into this friend zone to ensure that he has an opportunity to develop a deeper relationship if the opportunity should become available. Though early in our friendship I felt this way, as I matured and became closer to God, I had discerned that we were complements to each other's vision. Not only were we complements to each other's vision, but we also embodied key elements of the characters described in our visions.

One night as I pondered over what I wanted to do in my life, God revealed to me that Rainie would be my wife through a message He gave me. God spoke to my heart and told me that my vision of a successful family would occur in a relationship with her. Although he didn't say when, I knew in my heart that she would be my wife. In the excitement of the revelation I had received, I quickly prepared to ask Rainie to marry me. I had no wedding date planned and wasn't sure how long it would take to prepare; all I knew was that God said she would be my wife and she was what I desired.

After years of being engaged and taking premarital classes, our lives were in a prime place for change. At this point we were seasoned college students who had overcome many obstacles, while working together financially and pursuing God in ministry. We had made plans to marry and have a wedding the following year, but God was calling us to something drastic. Through prayer, God had revealed to us that instead of waiting for our scheduled wedding date, it was best to get married at that time.

In obedience to God, we decided nine months prior to our scheduled wedding date to get married. This act of obedience was big in our relationship. At that moment, we had decided that apart from what anyone thought, our goal was to do the will of God.

I knew that moments like that don't come around often; and when God says to move, you move in faith. This further confirmed that the good work that God was doing in me to prepare me to be a husband was for an expected time. Often, we make plans as to when and how we think things should be done; but when we allow God to prepare us to remain ready for His call, things always work out better in the end. I am positive that had I not been obedient to God in that moment, the wedding would not have been the same.

CONCLUSION

❖

Regardless of where you are in the process of life, know that God is faithful. When you surrender it all to Him, miraculous things will blossom in your life. First you must understand that you must be willing to obey God to answer the call on your life.

God is calling you to go higher in your life; and in order to transform into greatness, you must be willing to shed some people, places and things. You must be willing to let go and let God in. Just as a butterfly has four stages--the egg, the caterpillar, pupa and the butterfly--a woman has transitional stages in preparation of becoming a wife. The goal isn't getting married; the goal is staying married, and if you aren't properly developed for that position, the trials of marriage may destroy you.

I want to personally thank you for reading my book, "When God Sent My Husband", and I invite you to join the countless women all around the world in the "Love Class Book Club". Go to www.RainieHoward.com

From High School Prom to 12+ Years of Marriage

When I say all things are possible with God in your life I mean it. My husband & I both come from single parent homes. After being best friends, we started... More

10,062 Likes · 363 Comments · 819 Shares

After being best friends, we started dating my senior year of high school. During the last years of college, when my husband was 20 years old & I was 21 we got married. Although we knew it would be challenging we worked together to build a strong marriage, finish school and start our careers and have kids. We've been through so many tests and trials.

We have laughed, cried, argued, and had lots of fun together! After two master degrees, three businesses and amazing careers our teamwork has paid off. We started off with a one-bedroom apartment to now living in a five bedroom two-story home. God has blessed us with two amazingly smart children we love dearly.

We've experienced so much in the 15 years we've known each other. In the beginning so many people didn't believe we would make it. They said we were too young and dumb. We were broke and naïve…BUT God! God has been in the center of it all. Whenever we encounter difficult moments we pray for direction and provision, we never go to bed angry and our love has grown stronger & stronger. I write all of this to encourage you not to give up on love. The union of

"Marriage" is under an attack and so many people have lost their faith in being happily married. So many people don't believe love exist especially in young people. We are here to display true unconditional LOVE! Don't give up on experiencing real love; it's so POWERFUL! I never knew love like this was real.

P.S. We did this with no infidelity, no affairs and no other relationships. All men don't cheat, there are faithful men and women still living, breathing and loving in this world. There is HOPE!

#RealLoveExist
Join The Movement!

1. SHARE YOUR MARRIAGE LOVE STORY BY CLICKING BELOW "SHARE STORY"

2. POST, TWEET, PIN, SNAP & WIN. GET CREATIVE & SHARE YOUR STORY & BOOK IMAGES USING #RealLoveExist

*WINNERS DRAWN MONTHLY

Made in the USA
Charleston, SC
20 October 2016